AWESOME AGRICULTURE

SOYBEANS

an A-to-Z book

Susan Anderson & JoAnne Buggey

Book design by Nancy Roberts

Northwest Arm Press

• •

This book is dedicated to Bob

• •

Northwest Arm Press, Inc.
540 Southgate Drive, Suite 204
Bedford Nova Scotia Canada B4A 0C9
www.AgBooksForKids.com

Tractor illustrations by Gerry Cleary,
    from an original idea by James Jahoda
Project photographer: Lisa Marie Noseworthy,
    LMNO Photo
Fact-checking and proofreading: Paddy Muir

Models:
    L & Z: Ruth Riley
    O: Dillon Carter
    T, Z, & activities: Cohen Anthony Haines Dowden

Printed in the United States of America
Third printing

Library and Archives Canada Cataloguing in Publication

Anderson, Susan, 1950-
    Awesome agriculture : soybeans : an A-to-Z book /
    Susan Anderson & JoAnne Buggey.

(Awesome agriculture for kids)
ISBN 978-0-9811335-1-5

    1. Soybean--Juvenile literature. 2. Soybean products--
    Juvenile literature.
I. Buggey, JoAnne II. Title. III. Title: Soyabeans. IV. Series:
    Awesome agriculture for kids

SB205.S7A53 2009   j633.3'4   C2009-901111-5

Hello!

I'm Agri-Culture. Call me Agri.

You will see me on every page of this book about soybeans.

Each page contains

- A letter of the alphabet
- A word about soybeans beginning with that letter
- A picture and information to help you understand the word
- ME to help you learn more about each word

Let's start with **Aa** on the next page...

Aa

This is a field of soybeans.

agriculture

Agriculture is awesome. Soybeans are a part of agriculture.

Bb

Does your school bus use biodiesel?

biodiesel

Trucks and buses can use fuel made from soybeans.
It is called biodiesel.

Cc

Do you have a favorite candy? Check the label to see if it has soy in it. The label might read "soy lecithin."

candy

Soybeans are in much of the candy you eat.

Dd

dog food

There are soybeans in many kinds of dog food.

Do you have any pets that have soy in their food?

Ee

The environment is very important to soybean farmers. They care about your future.

environment

Soybean farmers take good care of the environment.

Ff

Farmers plant soybeans in the spring.

field

This farmer is planting soybeans in a field.

Gg

Look for soy foods at your grocery store.

grocery store

A grocery store has many foods made from soy.

Hh

Soybeans are harvested in the fall.

harvest

The combine is harvesting the soybeans.

Ii

This is a logo for soy ink.

ink

Many newspapers are printed with soy ink.

Jj

Maybe some day you will have a job working with soybeans.

jobs

Many people have jobs working with soybeans.

Kk

know

Did you know these things are made with soybeans?

Ll

lotions

Some hand lotions have soybean oil in them.

Mm

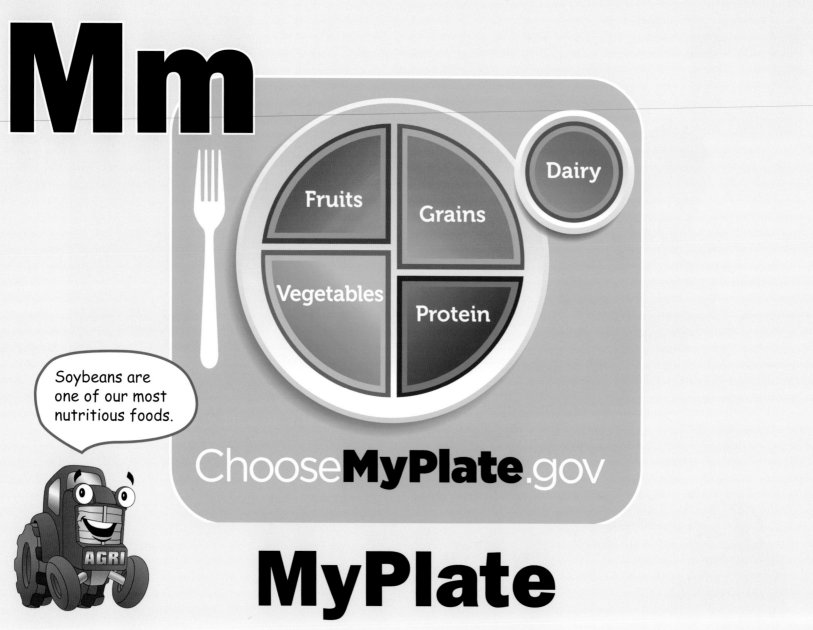

MyPlate

Soybeans can count either as a Vegetable or as Protein.

Nn

Soybeans make healthy foods because they are high in protein, fiber, and many vitamins and minerals.

nutrition

People and animals all over the world use soybeans for good nutrition.

Oo

Ask how soybean oil is used where you live.

oil

Many people cook with soybean oil.

Pp

A soybean plant usually grows to be about 36 inches tall. How tall are you?

36"

24"

12"

0

plants

These are soybean plants. The soybeans grow in pods.

Qq

High quality means the soybeans are the best they can be.

quality

Soybean farmers want to grow high-quality beans.

Rr

research

Many people are doing research to find new uses for soybeans.

Ss

This is the size of a soybean.

soybeans

These are soybeans.

Tt

People around the world eat tofu. It can be used to make a great smoothie.

tofu

Have you ever tried tofu? It is made from soybeans.

Uu

Are soybeans grown in your state? The top soybean-producing states are Illinois, Indiana, Iowa, Minnesota, and Nebraska.

United States

The states colored yellow grow most of the soybeans.

Vv

Talk to your doctor about vitamins at your next checkup.

vitamins

You can get important vitamins from soyfoods.

Vitamins help keep you heathy.

Ww

A soybean farmer watches temperature, rainfall, and other weather conditions.

AGRI

weather

Weather is very important to soybean producers.

Xx

INGREDIENTS:
WHEAT FLOUR, MALT,
WATER, SALT, CERTIFIED
ORGANIC SOYBEAN OIL
AND YEAST. X

Look for soy on the labels of products that you use.

x marks the spot

Find X on this label. It shows that there is soy in the product.

Yy

These are my favorite pages about soybeans. What are yours?

Ff
field
This farmer is planting soybeans in a field.

Farmers plant soybeans in the spring.

Cc
candy
Soybeans are in much of the candy you eat.

Do you have a favorite candy? Check the label to see if it has soy in it. Hint: it might say "soy lecithin."

Oo
oil
Many people cook with soybean oil.

Ask how soybean oil is used where you live.

you

What did you like best about soybeans?

Zz

Z to A or A to Z

Soybeans are awesome! We all agree.

activities

Make a smoothie!

You could make this soy drink. Ask an adult to help you. Here is the recipe:

Strawberry Banana Smoothie

3 cups vanilla soy milk
1 cup strawberries
1 banana

Mix in blender until smooth. To make it frothy use frozen strawberries. Serves 4.

- Look for 10 other facts that you like about soybeans.

- Ask an adult to help you find which states have activities for kids on their soybean websites.

- Make a song or write a poem about soybeans.

- Collect labels that include soybean products. How many can you find?

The Awesome Agriculture A-to-Z series

SOYBEANS, an A-to-Z book, 2009
American Farm Bureau Federation
2010 PreK-K Accurate Ag Book

PIGS, an A-to-Z book, 2010

CORN, an A-to-Z book, 2011

BEEF CATTLE, an A-to-Z book, 2013

For children 8–11
The Story of Agriculture series

SOYBEANS in the Story of Agriculture
American Farm Bureau Federation
2010 Book of the Year

PIGS & PORK in the Story of Agriculture, 2010

CORN in the Story of Agriculture, 2012

BEEF CATTLE in the Story of Agriculture, 2013

Both soybean books are also Illinois Ag in the Classroom 2010 Ag Week Books of the Year. Soybeans in the Story of Agriculture is also Minnesota Farm Bureau 2010 Book of the Year.

The Authors

JoAnne Buggey has a PhD in Curriculum & Instruction from the University of Washington (1971). She taught future elementary teachers in the College of Education and Human Development at the University of Minnesota. JoAnne has written dozens of textbooks for children including an American history text, *America! America!* and a civics text, *Civics for Americans.* Her recent multimedia projects include Exploring Where and Why, a program on maps and mapping for grades K–3.

Susan Anderson earned her MS in Curriculum & Instruction from Minnesota State University, Mankato (1988). She is an Education Specialist for University of Minnesota Extension and in the College of Food, Agricultural and Natural Resource Sciences. Susan grew up on a farm and lives on a working farm today. During her elementary teaching years she developed an interdisciplinary fifth-grade curriculum to increase agricultural literacy.

Both authors have been elementary teachers in the Minneapolis Public Schools. They currently work with the K-12 Education Program at the University of Minnesota Southwest Research and Outreach Center at Lamberton. They provide workshops for future and current elementary teachers in agricultural literacy. Both have contributed to curriculum projects including materials related to dairy and pigs. The authors serve on various boards related to agriculture and have won awards for quality teaching about agriculture. JoAnne and Susan are currently part of an Improving Teacher Quality grant team.

Acknowledgements

For invaluable assistance, warm thank-yous to Brenda Riley; Selina Water Eagle; Naomi Mortensen and Sam Ziegler at Minnesota Soybean Research & Promotion Council; Robert Anderson, Minnesota soybean producer and farm financial manager; Abby L. Stutsman, Osborn & Barr.

Image Credits